Global Issues

Clean Air and Water

Cheryl Jakab

Smart Apple Media

This edition first published in 2008 in the United States of America by Smart Apple Media.
All rights reserved. No part of this book may be reproduced in any form or by any means without written permission from the publisher.

Smart Apple Media
2140 Howard Drive West
North Mankato, Minnesota 56003

First published in 2007 by
MACMILLAN EDUCATION AUSTRALIA PTY LTD
627 Chapel Street, South Yarra, Australia 3141

Visit our Web site at www.macmillan.com.au or go directly to www.macmillanlibrary.com.au

Associated companies and representatives throughout the world.

Copyright © Cheryl Jakab 2007

Library of Congress Cataloging-in-Publication Data

Jakab, Cheryl.
    Clean air and water / by Cheryl Jakab.
    p. cm. — (Global issues)
    Includes index.
    ISBN 978-1-59920-122-1
    . Air—Pollution. 2. Water—Pollution. I. Title.

    TD883.J3756 2007
    363.73—dc22

                                                2007004555

Edited by Anna Fern
Text and cover design by Cristina Neri, Canary Graphic Design
Page layout by Domenic Lauricella and Cristina Neri
Photo research by Legend Images
Illustrations by Andrew Louey; maps courtesy of Geo Atlas

Printed in U.S.

Acknowledgements

The author and the publisher are grateful to the following for permission to reproduce copyright material:

Front cover inset photograph: Industrial effluent from a detergent factory flowing into the River Thames, Essex, England, © Photolibrary/Science Photolibrary. Earth photograph courtesy of Photodisc.

Background photograph of Earth and magnifying glass image both courtesy of Photodisc.

© age fotostock/Claver Carroll, pp. 7 (bottom), 25; © age fotostock/Javier Larrea, p. 14; The Australian National University, p. 19; BigStockPhoto, pp. 10, 24, 28; © Dreamshot63/Dreamstime.com, p. 5; Paul Harris/Fairfaxphotos, p. 26; © Slawek Schubert /Fotolia, pp. 6 (top), 20; © Stuart Taylor/Fotolia, p. 21; Uzi Keren/Getty Images, pp. 6 (bottom), 17; Guang Niu/Getty Images, pp. 7 (right), 9; © Scott Everett / iStockphoto.com, p. 8; Photolibrary/Science Photolibrary, pp. 6 (left), 12, 13, 15, 16, 22; Rob Cruse Photography, p. 27; © vixique/Shutterstock, p. 23; © WizData, inc./Shutterstock, p. 11.

Please note
At the time of printing, the Internet addresses appearing in this book were correct. Owing to the dynamic nature of the Internet, however, we cannot guarantee that all these addresses will remain correct.

Contents

Glossary words
When a word is printed in **bold**, you can look up its meaning in the glossary on page 31.

Facing global issues

Hi there! This is Earth speaking. Will you take a moment to listen to me? I have some very important things to discuss.

We must face up to some urgent environmental problems! All living things depend on my environment, but the way you humans are living at the moment, I will not be able to keep looking after you.

The issues I am worried about are:
- the huge number of people on Earth
- the supply of clean air and water
- wasting resources
- energy supplies for the future
- protecting all living things
- **global warming** and **climate change**

My global challenge to you is to find a **sustainable** way of living. Read on to find out what people around the world are doing to try to help.

Fast fact

In 2005, the **United Nations Environment Program** Report, written by experts from 95 countries, concluded that 60 percent of Earth's resources are being **degraded** or used unsustainably.

What's the issue?
Clean air and water

Everyone needs clean air and **fresh water** to survive. Polluted air and water can be damaging to health. Many human activities pollute the air and water around the world. Cleaning up this pollution is an urgent global environmental issue.

Air to breathe

People and other animals need clean air to breathe at all times. People can only survive for a few minutes without breathing air. Fortunately air is freely available in the **atmosphere**. Breathing polluted air causes lung damage and other diseases.

Water to drink

People are made of more than 70 percent water and need drinking water every day. Only a small amount of water on Earth is drinkable. Most water on Earth is salty water in oceans. Drinking water that is polluted has become a major cause of disease and even death.

Fast fact
The United Nations estimates that a quarter of all preventable illnesses are due to dirty drinking water.

Breathing polluted city air can cause lung damage and other illnesses.

Air and water issues

The most urgent air and water problems around the globe include:
- activities that pollute the air (see issue 1)
- activities that pollute the water (see issue 2)
- availability of safe drinking water (see issue 3)
- damage due to **acid rain** (see issue 4)
- overuse of fresh water (see issue 5)

ARCTIC OCEAN

Arctic Circle

NORTH

The Great Lakes

AMERICA

SOUTH

AMERICA

SOU

ATLA

OCE

ISSUE 2
The Great Lakes
Water pollution from industry. See pages 12–15.

ISSUE 3
The Middle East
Lack of access to fresh drinking water. See pages 16–19.

around the globe

ISSUE 4

Europe
Acid rain due to local and faraway air pollution. See pages 20–23.

EUROPE

The Middle East

China

Beijing

ASIA

AFRICA

ISSUE 1

Beijing
Smog and other air pollution problems. See pages 8–11.

Equator

H

T I C

N

AUSTRALIA

Tropic of Capricorn

ISSUE 5

Australia
People are using too much fresh water. See pages 24–27.

NTARCTICA

7

Polluting the air

Polluted air is a danger to health. Substances that pollute the air include tiny pieces of solid materials, called particulate matter, and poisonous gases. These come mainly from burning coal, oil, and other **fossil fuels** to power transportation and industry.

Air pollutants

Many air pollutants can be damaging to health. The **World Health Organization** publishes air quality guidelines showing the levels of pollutants that are damaging to health such as:

- particulate matter
- sulfur dioxide
- nitrous oxides
- hydrocarbons
- carbon monoxide
- lead
- ozone
- radon

Fast fact

In December 1952, air pollution in the city of London produced a killer smog that caused the death of 4,000 people immediately and perhaps another 8,000 more in the following weeks. The pollution was due mainly to burning coal.

Health problems

Asthma, bronchitis, and lung cancer are some of the **respiratory diseases** caused by air pollution. In many cities today, weather reports include air-pollution warnings. These describe expected pollution levels and suggest when people with breathing problems should avoid physical activity.

Los Angeles (pictured), Mexico City, Beijing, and many other major cities regularly suffer from severe air pollution.

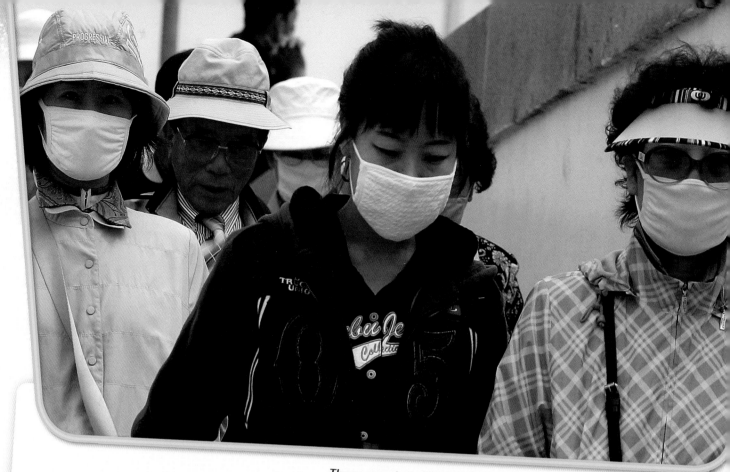

These people in Beijing, in 2006, are wearing masks after a dust storm blanketed the city in a thin layer of sand.

CASE STUDY
Beijing

Beijing is the second largest industrial center in China. Beijing has serious problems with air pollution. The city's air is particularly bad due to heavy pollution from industry and dust storms.

Sources of pollution

Coal is the main fuel used in Beijing, and in most other Chinese cities. Many industries that burn coal are located within the city. The level of air pollutants from these factories has gone uncontrolled for many years. Added to this industrial pollution is an increasing number of cars being used for transportation in Beijing.

Erosion of soil from farmland around the city adds a great deal of dust to the air in Beijing during the drier times of the year.

Movement of pollution

When the wind blows, the air pollution from industry in Beijing quickly moves away from the city. However, when the weather is still, the pollutants are trapped over the city making the air dangerous to breathe.

Toward a sustainable future: Improving air quality

Air quality can be improved by:
- reducing pollutants going into the air
- locating polluting industries away from cities

Reducing pollutants

The amount of pollution from industry and cars can be reduced. Car exhaust fumes can be reduced by keeping car engines running well, and by using cars less. Technology is being developed to clean waste gases from factories to remove dangerous substances before the waste gases are released into the air.

Moving industry

Even with the best technology, factories still release some pollutants. One solution for reducing pollution in cities is to move industries away from high-population areas. Moving industry away is particularly important in areas where air movement cannot carry pollutants away.

Fast fact

China is aiming to greatly improve air quality in Beijing before it hosts the 2008 Olympic Games.

Moving industry away from residential areas improves city air quality and public health.

CASE STUDY
Car alternatives

Private cars, which burn petroleum, are the major cause of air pollution in many cities. Cities around the globe are introducing rules to reduce car use:

- London is limiting cars entering the downtown area
- Tokyo has fast, efficient and regular public transportation
- Los Angeles is encouraging bike riding or walking

Public transportation

Public transportation can carry more people more efficiently than private cars. In Tokyo, Japan, millions of people are moved quickly into and out of the city each day on public transportation. Fast, reliable public transportation systems mean fewer traffic jams and less air pollution.

Fast fact
In the city of Davis, in California, about 40 percent of people use bicycles as their main transportation. In the 1960s, Davis was the first city in the U.S. to paint bike lanes on streets.

Bicycle use

Bicycles are a nonpolluting form of transportation. Bicycle awareness programs and bicycle paths encourage people to think of the bicycle as an alternative to the car.

Riding a bike like these commuters in China keeps you fit and does not add to air pollution.

11

Polluting the water

Pollution is found in all types of water environments on Earth, including oceans, lakes, rivers, **groundwater**, and ice fields. Polluted water is unfit for use by people and other living things and can cause disease.

Pollutants in waterways can cause uncontrolled growth of **algae**, which can drastically reduce the amount of oxygen in the water, killing fish and other life forms.

Sources of pollution

Sources of pollution in waterways include:

- untreated **sewage**, or human waste, released into waterways
- oil spills that occur when the oil is mined and transported
- fertilizers used on crops being washed into waterways
- other toxic chemicals, such as pesticides, used to kill insects on food crops
- **eroded** soil and rock being washed into waterways
- **radioactive** wastes from uranium mining and nuclear power plants

Oil pollution

Oil pollution is an increasing problem for ocean and coastal wildlife. Even small amounts of oil spread rapidly to form deadly oil slicks. Because oil and water do not mix, the oil floats on the water and then washes up on large areas of coast.

Waste from a detergent factory flows into the Thames River, in Essex, England.

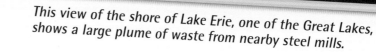

This view of the shore of Lake Erie, one of the Great Lakes, shows a large plume of waste from nearby steel mills.

CASE STUDY

The Great Lakes, North America

The Great Lakes are the largest expanse of fresh water in the world. Since the 1960s, pollution from phosphorus and the buildup of other toxic substances has become a major problem in five large lakes that make up the Great Lakes.

Phosphorus pollution

Phosphorus pollution in the Great Lakes came from fertilizers and human waste. Phosphorus increases the growth of plants. After a period of rapid growth, the plants die. As they die and decay, oxygen levels in the water fall, killing many fish and other living things in the water.

Fast fact
Together the Great Lakes hold about 20 percent of the world's fresh surface water.

Toxic chemicals

Today, in many areas around the Great Lakes, people are warned not to eat fish because they contain toxic substances. Toxic chemicals such as pesticides and industrial pollutants are killing life in the lakes.

Toward a sustainable future: Improving water quality

The main way to improve water quality is to decrease the amount of pollution going into the water. This can be done by:

- factories and towns treating their own waste
- preventing and promptly cleaning up oil spills

Treating wastes

Septic systems and traditional sewage treatment plants sometimes leak untreated waste into waterways. In **developing countries**, 95 percent of untreated waste flows into nearby rivers.

Human waste from towns that is treated and used as fertilizer is better than current methods which lead to water pollution. Industrial waste should have toxic substances removed at the factory before release of any waste water.

Oil spills

Oil companies can try to avoid oil spills during drilling and transportation of oil, but accidents will always happen. Some oil spill treatments, such as chemically sinking the oil, do not really solve the problem. New techniques try to clean up oil spills quickly and spare the natural environment.

Fast fact
For every million tons of oil that is shipped, about one ton is spilled.

Soldiers dressed in protective clothing clean up an oil spill from a tanker on the coast of Spain in 2002.

Worms can break down human waste into useful fertilizer.

CASE STUDY
Worm waste treatment

A sustainable alternative to city sewage plants is the use of worms to **recycle** human waste. The city of Brisbane, Australia, is using worm waste treatment with great success.

Worm composting

Earthworms can feed on human waste in the same way that they feed on scraps in a home compost bin. When the worms are kept in the right conditions, the waste material they feed on is changed into safe, useful worm castings.

Advantages of worm farming

Processing human waste in a worm farm has many advantages over traditional systems that use water to treat and carry waste away. Worm waste treatment keeps the human waste away from waterways and saves on water. The worm castings are also a useful fertilizer.

Fresh drinking water

People in many places around the world live without good quality drinking water. Particularly where there is extreme poverty, getting enough fresh water can be very difficult. Water good enough to drink is an urgent need around the world, particularly in Africa, the Middle East, and parts of Latin America.

Freshwater supplies

In the year 2000, it was estimated four out of five people living in towns did not have clean, fresh water. Very little of Earth's fresh water is suitable for humans to drink—about 8 out of every 10,000 gallons. Most fresh water is used in culture and industry, with less than 10 percent used in homes.

Fast fact
About 10 million people die from drinking contaminated water each year.

Water and disease

Water-related diseases are the single largest cause of death throughout the world. Drinking unsafe, or **contaminated**, water causes diseases such as cholera, diarrhea, and typhoid.

These girls in Mali, Africa, are washing dishes in river water.

Thousands of Palestinians in the West Bank region have no fresh water in their villages, and depend on Israel for water.

CASE STUDY

Water in the Middle East

The Middle East is an area in southwest Asia and northeast Africa that is largely **desert**. The Middle East is very dry and contains a number of different countries, cultures, and religions.

Scarce water resources

In the Middle East, water is a scarce resource that creates conflict among countries, including Israel, Jordan, Lebanon, and Saudi Arabia.

- Some of Israel's water supplies come from waterways diverted from Lebanon.
- Israel's use of ground and surface water is reducing groundwater supplies in Jordan.
- Saudi Arabia is rapidly emptying underground water sources, or aquifers, by overuse.

Sharing supplies

When people need to share water from the same source it can lead to conflicts. If a person, town, or country upstream takes water for their own use, downstream rivers can be reduced or run dry. Building dams across rivers can reduce the water flow, leaving little for people and other living things downstream.

Toward a sustainable future: Ensuring freshwater supplies

Today, most towns and cities in **developed countries** are supplied with reliable water "on tap." For a sustainable future, every person needs access to a steady supply of good quality drinking water.

Water for everyone

Treating and piping stored water from dams and rivers is just one way to provide water that is safe to drink. To make water available to everyone in every region, other technologies must be made available. Other techniques include desalination, rainwater tanks, and purifying contaminated water.

Collecting rainwater

Where large-scale piped water is not possible, rain falling onto buildings can be caught. Rainwater is a good source of clean drinking water in most areas, except for the driest areas on Earth, and in places where air pollution is a problem.

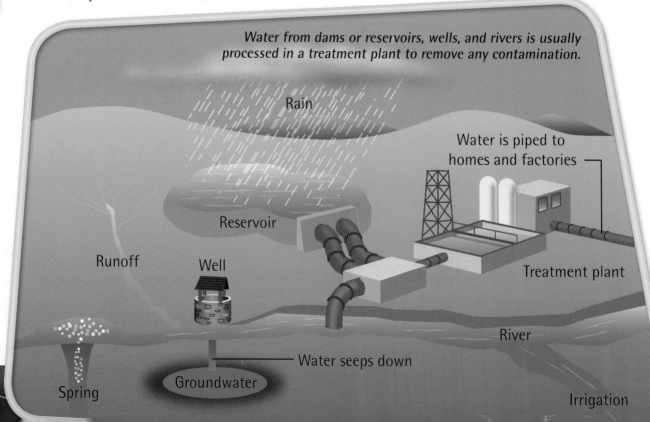

Water from dams or reservoirs, wells, and rivers is usually processed in a treatment plant to remove any contamination.

Rain

Water is piped to homes and factories

Reservoir

Runoff

Well

Treatment plant

River

Water seeps down

Spring

Groundwater

Irrigation

This simple filter could provide clean water to millions of people.

CASE STUDY
Ceramic filters

Water filters are simple devices that can clean dirty water to make it drinkable. A new water filter made from **ceramic** was recently developed by Australian scientist and potter Tony Flynn. Made from clay, the filter can be made by anyone and used anywhere.

How ceramic filters work

When water is slowly dripped through a ceramic filter, any unwanted material is left behind in the filter. This filter has been shown to remove common disease organisms.

Simple to make

Unlike other water filtering devices, Flynn's are simple and inexpensive to make. The filters are also very simple to explain and demonstrate.

This filter is made from clay from the ground that is mixed with straw. These materials are commonly available in developing countries. The filter is then hardened into ceramic by heating it on a fire fueled by animal manure.

Ceramic filters do not require any complex technology, and allow anyone in the world to drink water safely.

Acid rain

In the past, rain was a source of fresh water. Today, however, rain from polluted skies can be damaging acid rain.

Pollutants cause acid rain

The main pollutants causing acid rain are now known to be sulfur dioxide and nitrous oxides. Over the past 200 years, the atmosphere has steadily filled with these chemicals from burning fossil fuels used to provide power for industry and cars.

When these chemicals mix with moisture in the atmosphere, they form sulfuric acid and nitric acid. These acids are the destructive substances in acid rain.

Damage from acid rain

In the 1970s, damage from acid rain was first seen in the forests of Europe. It was then spread by air currents over most of the Northern Hemisphere, including Canada and the United States.

Acid rain burns or kills plants in forests and crops, and can lead to the death of many creatures in lakes and rivers. In cities, it damages building stones, metals, paints, tiles, ceramics, leather, and rubber.

This forest in Poland has been damaged by acid rain.

CASE STUDY
Damage to ancient monuments

Acid rain has eroded the surfaces of many great treasures, including ancient sculptures in Egypt, Greece, and Rome. The Sphinx, in Egypt, is one of the best known of all the ancient monuments that has now been damaged by acid rain.

Acid rain damages stone

Building stones, including marble, limestone, and sandstone, are all easily broken down by acid rain. The acid rain reacts with minerals in these stones, changing it from hard rock to soft powder.

Fast fact
The ancient Greek Acropolis is believed to have crumbled more in the last 40 years than it has in the previous 2,500 years.

Acid rain has damaged treasures that have stood for thousands of years, such as the Sphinx in Giza, Egypt.

Lost treasures

Other treasured buildings and monuments being damaged by acid rain include the Acropolis in Greece, Egyptian temples at Karnak, and the United States' Statue of Liberty. In England, St. Paul's Cathedral, Westminster Abbey, and Lincoln Cathedral have all been damaged by acid rain.

Toward a sustainable future: Reducing acid rain

It is now known that the main way to reduce acid rain is to cut levels of pollution from factories. The first controls were put in place before the processes that caused acid rain were fully understood by science.

Reducing emissions

In 1988, the "Long-Range Trans-boundary Air Pollution Agreement" was signed by 25 nations. The agreement put strict controls on sulfur dioxide **emissions** by industry. By 1999, Europe and North America appeared to be recovering from the damage done by acid rain.

Nations working together

Acid rain from air pollution spreads with air currents, so its effects can be felt some distance from the source of the pollution. When nations worked together and agreed to stop the cause of the problem, acid rain was reduced throughout most of the Northern Hemisphere, where it has had the worst effect.

Fast fact

In the 1990s, industry in China increased greatly and so has pollution and acid rain. Nearly 40 percent of China's land area is now affected by acid rain.

The yellowing needles of this tree have been damaged by acid rain.

CASE STUDY
The battle to save the Black Forest

When damage was first seen in trees of the Black Forest, the chemical reactions forming acid rain were not well understood. Various groups had different opinions on what to do.

Wait-and-see attitude

Changing the industries that were being blamed for acid rain would be costly. People in industry suggested that more scientific studies were needed to find out what was really happening. They wanted to wait and see more information before taking action.

Taking early precautions

The other side of the argument was that, even though acid rain was not fully understood, precautions should be taken immediately to try to help the forests. It made sense to stop factories from polluting the air, just in case this was the cause of acid rain.

In the end, it was shown that acid rain did come from industrial pollution, and that delaying action would make things worse. Today, the Black Forest is much healthier due to the changes that were made to reduce pollution.

The Black Forest is growing back due to strict controls on air pollution.

Overuse of water

Overuse of our limited freshwater supplies has become an urgent global concern. People in developed countries use on average 10 times more water each day than people in developing countries.

Limited supply of fresh water

Freshwater supplies are limited and precious. The original source of all fresh water is rain. The amount of fresh water that is available depends on the rainfall. Groundwater comes from rain that has filtered down through the soil over a long time. Supplies cannot easily be increased.

Desalination

Desalination is the removal of salt from seawater to produce fresh drinking water. The cost of desalination is too high to make this an alternative source of fresh water in most places. Desalination can increase water supplies a little, but it does not solve the problem of people wasting water.

Fast fact
People in Asia, Africa, Central America, and South America use 13 to 26 gallons of water per day, while some people in North America use 106 to 132 gallons per day.

Keeping lawns green uses a great deal of water in dry climates.

This rice crop in New South Wales, Australia, is watered by irrigation.

CASE STUDY
Water use in Australia

Australia is the driest inhabited continent in the world. Two-thirds of the country is desert or semi-desert. There are few permanent rivers, and water supplies are very limited.

Despite this, Australians are among the biggest users of fresh water in the world. In 2005, the average amount of water used per person in Australia was about 83 gallons (314 l) per day. Water **consumption** in Australia increased greatly through the 1980s and 1990s.

Irrigation

Irrigation has been vital in the development of agriculture in Australia. Most of Australia's irrigation water comes from underground sources such as the Great Artesian Basin.

However, many irrigation methods waste precious water supplies. In Australia, irrigation water is mostly carried in open channels. Leakage and evaporation by the sun cause a great deal of water to be lost from these channels.

Fast fact
In 2006, the International Environmental Performance Index ranked Australia 119th out of 133 nations in water conservation measures.

Toward a sustainable future: Water conservation

Conserving precious water supplies will ensure that there will be ongoing supplies for the future. To conserve water, we need to reduce the amount of water used, especially in places where there is little rainfall.

Measures to conserve water and to stop overuse can include:

- using less water by thinking about where savings can be made
- reusing water, for example, by watering gardens with kitchen and laundry water
- recycling used water by purifying it for reuse
- decreasing evaporation, including piping water and holding it in closed tanks rather than in open reservoirs

Using less

Using less water requires people in homes, industry, and agriculture to think about water conservation as a responsibility. When water flows freely by turning a faucet, it is easy to overuse. Adopting simple measures to make many little savings each day can save large amounts of water.

This family gets all the water they use in their house and garden from rainwater falling on their roof.

Rainwater tanks can collect water from any roof.

CASE STUDY
Catching rainwater

Catching rainwater off the roofs of houses can add a great deal to the freshwater supplies that are available. Some people living in Australian cities have shown they can catch all the rainwater they need for a whole year.

Installing rainwater tanks

Households in the middle of large cities are now installing water tanks. Having a water tank to collect rainwater from the house roof has a long history in Australia. Rain falling on the roof runs through downspouts into the tank.

Perhaps in the future, all houses will have rainwater tanks. Small tanks that are used for watering the garden are now becoming common in many Australian cities since regulations on using town water supplies in gardens are enforced.

What can you do?
Save water and reduce air pollution

You may think that just one person cannot do much, but everyone can help. If every person is careful, the little differences can add up.

Prevent air pollution

You can make a difference in the quality of the air by:

- reducing your reliance on the car
- walking or riding a bike for short trips
- using public transportation when it is available
- reducing the use of heating that can add to air pollution

Walking or riding a bike to school does not add to air pollution.

Fast fact
A slow dripping tap loses about a gallon (four l) of water an hour.

Use less water

You can make a difference in water use by:

- having shorter showers
- turning off the faucet while brushing teeth
- reusing bath water in the washing machine or garden
- catching clean kitchen water to use in the garden
- fixing dripping or leaky faucets
- installing water-saving showerheads, faucets, and toilets

Conduct a water audit

On average, showers make up about 16 percent of the average household water use in the U.S. That's about 4,200 gallons (19,090 l) per house per year.

What to do

- Time the length of your shower (in minutes).
- Collect water as you usually have it flowing in the shower in a bucket for 10 seconds.
- Measure the amount of water collected in the bucket.
- Work out how much comes out in one minute. (Multiply the amount you collected by six.)
- Multiply the length of your shower by the amount that comes out each minute.

How much water do you use each day, in a week, and in a year?

Toward a sustainable future

Well, I hope you now see that if you accept my challenge your world will be a better place. There are many ways to work toward a sustainable future. Imagine it . . . a world with:

- a stable climate
- clean air and water
- nonpolluting, **renewable** fuel supplies
- plenty of food
- resources for everyone
- healthy natural environments

This is what you can achieve if you work together with my natural systems.

We must work together to live sustainably. That will mean a better environment and a better life for all living things on Earth, now and in the future.

Web sites

For further information on air and water quality, visit these Web sites:

- GreenHome acfonline.org.au/default.asp?section_id=86
- Planet Ark www.planetark.com
- Worm waste treatment www.wormdigest.org

acid rain
rain containing acids which falls from polluted skies

algae
living things that are found in water and make food using the energy from the sun

atmosphere
the layer of gases surrounding Earth

ceramic
hard material such as pottery, porcelain, and bricks, made by heating materials from the earth, such as clays, to high temperatures

climate change
changes to the usual weather patterns in an area

consumption
amount used or consumed

contaminated
polluted with unwanted substances

degraded
run-down or reduced to a lower quality

desert
area of low plant cover and low rainfall

developed countries
countries with industrial development, a strong economy, and a high standard of living

developing countries
countries with less developed industry, a poor economy, and a lower standard of living

emissions
substances that are released into the environment

eroded
area where rock and soil have been broken down and carried away by wind and water

fossil fuels
fuels such as oil, coal, and gas, which formed underground from the remains of animals and plants that lived millions of years ago

fresh water
water low enough in salt and other chemicals to be suitable for drinking

global warming
an increase in the average temperature on Earth

groundwater
water found below the surface of the land

radioactive
material that produces waves of energy, called radiation

recycle
reprocess a material so that it can be used again

renewable
a resource that can be constantly supplied and which does not run out

respiratory diseases
diseases of the lungs and airways used for breathing

sewage
human wastes

smog
thick air pollution from burning coal combined with fog

sustainable
a way of living that does not use up natural resources

United Nations Environment Program
a program, which is part of the United Nations, set up to encourage nations to care for the environment

World Health Organization
a section of the United Nations that deals with public health

Index